BUSINESS PLAN WRITING GUIDE

HOW TO WRITE A SUCCESSFUL & SUSTAINABLE BUSINESS PLAN IN UNDER 3 HOURS

ClydeBank
BUSINESS

Copyright © 2014
ClydeBank Media LLC
www.clydebankmedia.com
All Rights Reserved

ISBN-13 : 978-1502771414

CONTENTS

INTRODUCTION

First, I would like to commend you for having the initiative, drive, vision and passion for creating your own business. The majority of people in this world will go about their lives working for someone else and will never own anything of their own. By purchasing this book, you have shown that you are ready to put your idea for a business into motion and start a real life, profitable, sustainable business.

This process can be overwhelming for most people and many can fall into a "paralysis by analysis" situation, where they do not take the necessary actions to start their business simply because they don't know how. This book will shed light on this process and will teach you how to write business plans that can turn a great idea into an amazing business.

I'll start with the fundamentals, explain exactly why you need a business plan, when you should create it, and what information you'll need before you get started. From there, I will dive deeper into the specific chapters, or sections, of your plan and teach you the shortcuts that will allow you to generate this content quickly while not sacrificing quality.

Follow me into the world of entrepreneurship by creating your first million-dollar business plan today. See you inside.

CHAPTER ONE
Why, When & How?

Before you get into actually writing your business plan, it's important to understand all the questions you probably have about your business plan. Let's take a few minutes to answer all some questions before we dive into the actual writing of your business plan.

Who Needs a Business Plan?

This is a trick question, because everyone needs a business plan. If you are going into any type of business, you need a business plan. A new startup company that's just venturing out needs a business plan. An established business that's looking to expand needs a business plan. If you are in business and want to be successful you need a plan.

You will find that as a business owner, the business plan that you create in the beginning is helpful throughout your company's existence. Your plan grows and develops as your company grows and develops. You continually modify your business plan as your company changes through time.

Why Write a Business Plan?

First and foremost, research has shown that you are two and half times more likely to actually go into business if you take the time to write a business plan. With that alone in mind, it's probably worth writing a business plan. Why is this statistic true? Those who take the time to write business plans have proven that they are willing to take the extra steps to make running a business work. Business plans are used for a variety of reasons, but one of their main purposes is to show potential investors your business' overall goals and strategies.

Investors like to see all of your research in one neat and tidy document. They like knowing that you've done your research and have the ability to follow through with that research. A business plan shows that you can take all of your ideas and the research that you have done prior to talking with investors and put it down on paper in a nice, concise format. Many business owners will tell you that writing a business plan was essential for them, because it helped them organize their thoughts before they talked to investors and made any major business decisions. Business plans are a great tool to get you thinking about all the aspects of your business, which is one of reasons they are so valuable to write. You'll think about your marketing strategy and your finances, as well as your start-up costs, business management, and organization. Thinking through all of these individual details as you get started will take your big ideas and focus them into very specific areas. Writing a business plan is a vital tool for getting started with your business. It's a proven positive guide for getting your business off the ground and even required by many investors. Take the time to make sure your business plan is professional and well done.

When Should I Write My Business Plan?

Business plans are the tool that you use to organize your business. They are a way for you to take every idea that's floating around in your head and organize it in one place. For many people, it's a way to get key investors on board with your business, but your business plan is much more than that. If you need to employ several people other than yourself, your business plan can help to recruit those key employees to work for you.

So when should you write your business plan? Before you talk to investors, you are going to need a business plan. Before you are able to recruit employees to your business, you will need a business plan. You can also use your business plan to watch how your business progresses throughout the first weeks, months and years. If you project that your company will have certain profits by the end of a quarter or that you will have so many employees, you can check those things against your business plan. A business plan only works if it was created prior to your business starting its operations.

How Long Should My Business Plan Be?

Overall, business plans should be short and to the point. They should be straightforward and not overly wordy. Investors and possible employees don't want to waste incredible amounts of time reading through long documents, but they are interested in what you have to say. Make every sentence and every word count. Here are a few tips to making your business plan as effective as possible.

- **Consider Using Shorter Sentences.** Longer sentences are okay, but only if you really want to use them for a specific meaning. People multitask and may read your business plan while doing other things. They may also just skim through your business plan. Don't take it personallyIf your sentences are too long or complicated, key things you want to get across won't get picked up by the reader.

- **Avoid Using Acronyms,** jargon, or other words that only people in your field would know. If you feel that you need to, explain them briefly, so your reader can understand what it means. You can't always assume that your readers know the same things as you.

- **Use Bullet Points for Lists.** They will help your readers stay focused on what you are trying to get across and help to emphasize the most important things. It also helps the reader to easily go back and find information that was important or something that they want to reference again. When you have bullet points, don't just list things without giving an explanation. There is nothing more frustrating to a reader than to have a list, but no explanation to accompany the list. Make sure everything on your list is adequately explained, so your reader isn't left with questions.

- **Keep It Short.** The average business plan today is approximately forty pages long. You will have around 20-30 pages of regular text for all the parts of your business plan and then around ten pages of appendices. We will explain what all those entail later, but it's important to note that if your business plan ends up more than 40 pages, you should probably go back and see where you can cut back and summarize better.

- **Graphics Are The Exception.** When you add in lots of graphics to your business plan, it can add pages of length. If that happens, don't fret. You can still use the forty-page rule; just see how it measures without the graphics. You might find that you want to add graphics or pictures of your product, possible locations, menus, floor plans, logos, etc. All of these can be very useful; don't shy away from adding graphics just because it lengthens your business plan. Charts can do the same thing. Consider bar graphs or pie charts that can enhance the market comparisons or profit margins you are projecting. These are also valuable to your business plan.

- **Choose Your Font Wisely.** Perhaps this goes without saying, but use a very readable font that is standard. You can change the font for your headings, but stick to only two fonts for your whole document. Keep it simple.

- **Use Spellcheck and Proofread.** If grammar and punctuation aren't your strong point, have a friend or colleague do you a favor and review your plan. Make sure to double-check all your numbers, too. This is something that an outside proofreader can't check; it's your responsibility! The last thing you want is to be embarrassed when your figures don't add up for an investor.

Hopefully we've talked through some of your initial questions about business plans. It's important that you feel confident about writing your business plan before you get started.

CHAPTER TWO

Do Your Homework

Before you get started writing your own business plan, there's some homework to do. This is the part where you have to do your research and prepare it to outline your goals and objectives. Here are some important points to research as you do your homework.

Research Your Potential Markets

This is the research piece where you start to think and analyze who is going to actually use the products and/or services that you are going to be offering. This shouldn't be you just guessing or thinking through the potential market. You should actually hit the pavement and talk to potential customers and ask them questions. Conduct real interviews, collect data, and ask questions of people to whome you think you might actually be selling. One of the most important questions to ask yourself when you start is if there is a market for your product or service in your area. Hopefully the answer to this question is yes. If you truly believe there isn't a market for your product in your area, and you're passionate about opening your business, you'll have to consider relocating to an area where there is a market for your product or service. Think outside the box, because usually with a little creativity there is a market for just about anything. It just needs to be presented in the right way and marketed well..

After you have determined that there is a market for your product or service, you should ask further follow-up questions. Ask questions about age groups, gender, ethnicities, economic populations, etc. After analyzing the answers to these questions, think about whether your potential customers live in certain neighborhoods or certain areas of town more than others. Are you targeting kids or adults? Compile this data so you can easily access it later when you write your business plan. You can collect the data yourself, but sometimes it's better if someone else collects the data, because an outside source is unbiased. When you use a secondary source, people may be more willing to be honest instead of just telling you what they think you want to hear.

Regardless of how you choose to do your market research, this is one of the most important pieces of research. You will learn invaluable information that will guide you through the rest of the business planning process. Take your time and make sure you research your potential markets well and in great detail.

Determine Potential Market Size

When you begin, you probably have big dreams of becoming

extremely successful. Those dreams aren't impossible, but may need to realistically start small. Along with analyzing your market, you need to consider your market size and how many potential customers you have.

You might start out thinking that you have hundreds of thousands of potential customers, but that could be out of your reach at the beginning. Think of it this way: you've invented a new line of toothpaste – a product that everyone uses, right? So potentially, your market size could be the entire population of the world. That seems crazy and unthinkable now, but consider popular toothpaste brands that really do market to the entire world. They had to start somewhere, right? It is possible to get there, but you need to start with a smaller market size and work your way up to larger market sizes. Maybe start with toothpaste that specifically targets one group of people, like children, people with dentures, etc. After you've narrowed your market, you can start to ask yourself more specific questions about that market group:

- How many children need toothpaste in any given community?
- How many people with dentures live in the United States?
- How much toothpaste do people use in the course of a month or a year?
- Who else are you competing against in the toothpaste market?

By asking yourself these questions and other, similar questions , you can begin to learn where you fit in your market.

What Do You Need to Get Started?

Sit down and make a list of things you need to get yourself up and running as a company. Some of the things you need are simple and easy to obtain, like office supplies and computers, while others are much more complicated, like employees and product designs. At this point, don't be afraid to make the list as detailed as you need, not leaving anything out. You'll obviously need plenty of tangible things for your business to get off the ground, but there are plenty of intangible things, too, like market research and potential customers, to make it all come together.

This is the time for you to think through every step that needs to take place in order for your company to launch and all the things that could stand in the way of that happening.

Make Product Samples

Potential investors want to see the product or products they are investing in, so you'll need to have product samples to show off when you pitch your business plan. If you are offering a service instead of a product, be prepared to somehow demonstrate your service to them, either in person via a video demonstration. If you are opening a restaurant, invite potential investors for a meal and serve them a few dishes that will be on the menu. There are ample ways to show investors your products and services even if it isn't something they can't hold in their hands.

In addition, future employees will also be interested to see product samples and services. You will need to show them that yours is a company in which it's worth putting their time and effort. You are trying to convince these employees that your company is going to be successful, and they aren't going to be out looking for work in six months time. They also need to be excited about your product and services. They need to be selling the product as much as you are. If they are excited about the company, it will show in their daily work habits and their dedication to the company.

Initially your product samples may be homemade, and although that may work great, you want a product sample that says "wow" when you pull it out of the box. It should be attractive and flashy. Take your initial model and dress it up a little to impress your audience.

Find Possible Locations to Rent/Buy

It's time to go location hunting. Although you may not actually be renting out a space for a few months or more, you need to research what type of space you need. The only way you'll be able to do that is by actually seeing what you can get and how much the spaces cost.

Contact a real estate broker and have him or her walk you through several available retail spaces in neighborhoods where you are interested in locating your business. You will know these areas because you have already done your market research. Keep accurate records of all the places you see, so you know how much each location costs, the square footage, pictures, etc.

You will quickly learn what you can get for your money in each of your chosen neighborhoods and how that will affect your decisions. It will give you a good idea of the estimated monthly rent for your location.

A Quick Note

Rarely do novice business owners buy a location for their business, but it does happen (if you find a steal of deal or the perfect location). If you are interested in buying a location for your business, you can speak to your real estate broker about this as well. You will need to factor that into your start-up costs.

Figure Out Start-up Costs

Start-up costs aren't going to be pretty. This number will probably shock you in the beginning, but there are a couple of things to keep in mind. First, sit down and make a list of everything you need to get your business going. This is different from the list you made earlier, because this list only includes the things that cost money (it doesn't include the market research, the potential customers, etc.). Everything from cash registers and computers to industrial kitchen equipment and tables will need to be factored into the start-up costs.

You'll need to think about painting the walls, light fixtures, etc. at your new location. Try to be reasonable and conservative with your spending. Instead of going for the light fixtures that cost two hundred dollars apiece, see if you can find something discounted.

Cover the basics or the most important things first and then, down the road when you are turning a good profit, you can consider adding a few of the more expensive extras. Remember that right now you are just trying to get started, so don't go over the top. Research and see where you can find the best prices for things. There are plenty of places online that offer discounts for ordering in bulk. Since you will probably be ordering things in higher quantities, see if you can find these types of websites or stores. Build relationships with other local businesses that might offer your discounts if you buy their products in bulk as well. Here are a few things to remember when factoring in your start-up costs (there could be more, depending on your personal situation):

- Rent
- Utilities
- Salaries
- Equipment
- Maintenance for Equipment
- Supplies
- Legal Licenses or Permits
- Marketing and Promotion

Potential investors will want to see that you have researched and thought through your start-up costs, down to the very last paperclip. Make an organized chart, which breaks out each part of your start-up costs, so your investors can see how the money will be allocated. It is helpful for them to see this, because they don't want to just see that you'll need $100,000 to get started. They will need to see that it's not an unreasonable amount when break it down and show them where each dollar is going to be spent.

If you are struggling on how to get started estimating your start-up costs, there is a free online calculator that helps to break down your costs for the first six months. It helps to calculate and show your potential revenue as well. To find the online calculator, click Online Start-Up Costs Calculator

Who are Your Potential Investors?

You might have the best business idea in the world, but without the backing of a bank or investor(s), you aren't going to reach a single customer. People don't lend money just because you are a nice person or even because you have a good idea. There are specific guidelines that you have to meet in order for them to lend you money. Obviously if your idea is a good one, then you are well on your way, but you'll have to take it just a little further in order to secure yourself a loan and make your dream of owning a business a reality.

Banks and other lenders generally look at a potential business' capital, capacity, collateral, conditions, and character (the "5C's of lending"), in order to determine whether or not they will invest. Let's discuss what each of these 5C's mean to you, so you can prepare yourself and make sure you are ready when you talk with potential investors about your business.

Capital : This is basically what sources of income you have to repay the loan, other than the business you are trying to open. The bank wants to know if you lose your job, the business goes under, etc. there other ways of repayment for the loan, such as investments, savings, assets, etc.

Capacity : The bank will want to know how you handle debt and whether you can manage this new debt with your current income. They will judge this debt against any current debt you have. This called a debt-to-income ratio. They may judge this based on your former employment and any previous debt you may have had, and how you handled paying it off.

Collateral : This only applies if you are applying for a secured loan. A secured loan means that you are placing something as collateral against the loan. Think of an auto loan or a home equity loan. When you have those loans, there is a car or a house that the bank has as collateral against the loan. If you don't pay the loan back, the bank can come and take the car or house back. If you apply for a secured loan, you are offering something as collateral against the loan or at least part of the loan.

Conditions : The bank can ask how you plan to use the money they are loaning you. This can be very general or very specific, so be prepared to account for every dollar you are requesting. If you plan to purchase a vehicle for your business, they may want to know, and they may want to inspect the vehicle in order to approve the loan. A loan officer may be assigned to you and may place very specific conditions on your loan that you have to follow in order for the loan to be approved.

Character : This is also sometimes referred to as credit history instead of character, because the bank will pull your credit report and go over it will a fine tooth comb. They will want to know every detail of your credit history, and approval of your loan will be based on how your credit history looks to them. Have you defaulted on a loan before? Be prepared to defend yourself, because your track record is against you. Luckily credit history does improve with time, and if you defaulted years ago, it may not show up now.

If you are interested in seeing your credit score before you go to the bank, you can check your credit score for free. There are many imposter websites online, so be wary of giving out your personal information, The three credit report agencies, TransUnion, Equifax and Experian, are required by law to give you a free credit report once every twelve months.

Finding your potential investors and making sure that you are prepared with all the information you need to win them over is the key to getting your financing. Without financing, you obviously won't have a business, so make sure you're prepared and ready for their questions with product samples and a great business plan. Researching isn't the easiest thing, nor is it always the most fun, but it is vital to the success of your business plan. Now that you've done your research and you're prepared with all the right strategies, you are ready to start writing your actual business plan.

CHAPTER THREE

Executive Summary & Company Description

Now you're ready to start writing your business plan. The business plan itself has eight different parts, plus a possible ninth part - the appendix - for all the extra things that don't fit anywhere. We will explain each part of the business plan in detail; what should be included, how you should format it, how long it should be, etc. Let's get started.

Part 1: Executive Summary

The first piece of your business plan is the executive summary. Many people suggest leaving this piece until you've finished everything else. It is the most important part of your business plan, because it is the first thing anyone reads and the way those reading about your business get to know you. If you are just getting your thoughts organized, this isn't where you want to start. Start with Parts 2-8 and then come back to this when you feel more prepared to write this in an organized, professional manner. At the very least, if you choose to start here, commit to revisit this piece at least once, if not more, after you've finished your entire business plan to make sure you haven't changed things or modified certain pieces of your business plan.

What to Include in Your Executive Summary

This list is for both established businesses and start-ups. If you are a start-up/new business, you won't have as much information as an established business, or your information may be slightly different. Feel free to modify the information as necessary to fit your needs.

- **Mission Statement** : Take your time with this. It should be at least several sentences or a short paragraph, and it should describe your business objectives.

- **Company Information** : Include all the information you can about your business name, the founders, the number of employees, location(s), etc. (Established businesses will obviously have more information here.)

- **Company Growth** : Talk about how the company has grown since it first started, including profits, employees, market share, etc. (New businesses can leave this section out completely.)

- **Products/Services** : Take a couple sentences to talk about the products and/or services you will offer to customers. If you are an established business, talk about what you already offer and what you plan to offer in the future if you are expanding.

- **Financial Information** : If you are an established business, you'll need to include your current financial information (i.e., your bank or investors). It doesn't need to be too detailed, general information is fine. Again, new businesses do not need to include this section.

- **Brief Summary of Future Plans** : Talk about what your goals are for the business. Where do you see the business at the end of one year, five years, ten years, etc.

Start-ups don't have a lot of the information listed above, but focus on the information you do have. You can include information about your market analysis and why you believe your business will be successful in the area you've chosen. You can talk about how you feel that your product or service is filling a need in the community or in your particular target market. That will lead perfectly into your summary of your future plans.

The executive summary should only be a page, which means every single word you put in that page needs to be chosen carefully. Except for your mission statement, everything else is short, maybe a sentence or two. Your executive summary needs to grab your reader and pull them into your business, making them excited to learn more about what you are planning. You need to show how your business is going to be successful and sell every aspect of not only your business, but yourself.

Part 2: Company Description

This is the section where you actually pitch your business to your readers. In the previous section, you attracted their interest and enticed them to learn more about your business. This is the section where you deliver that description. Focus on these specific things in your company description.

- **Goals** : Talk about your specific goals for the company. You want to express your vision for the company and how you plan to make that vision a reality, without getting too detailed (that's what the rest of the business plan will outline).

- **What You're All About** : This is where you get to explain what makes your business unique and different from everyone else. If you're opening a smoothie shop, what makes your smoothie shop different from the hundreds of smoothie shops that already exist? Why should an investor look at your shop differently than the others? Give them a reason to love yours above the rest.

- **Marketplace Needs** : Briefly talk about marketplace needs you will accommodate with your product or service. This is where you discuss a hole you have found in the market that you believe needs to be filled. You will have a whole section of your business plan dedicated to talking about your market, so only briefly mention this here.

- **How Your Products or Services Meet the Needs** : After talking about how the marketplace has needs to befilled, you move into discussing how your products or services will fill that gap. This is where you look back at how you've described how your business is unique and different and match it with the need in the marketplace. As these two things fuse together, you establish how your business will be successful.

- **Who You Serve** : Next you want your readers to understand exactly to whom you are trying to sell your products or services; take the time to talk about your target customer. You've done your research, and you've already made this decision. You already know if you're targeting stay at home moms, children, or retired veterans. It's easy to plug this information in here.

- **How Will You Be Successful** : As you continue moving forward, you will need a few advantages over your competition, and your readers need to see them. What do you have up your sleeve? Here are a few advantages that you could have or look into as you continue in the planning process:

  - Key Location

  - Expert Employees

  - Efficient Operations

  - Ability to Operate Cheaper *(if this is your advantage, be prepared to explain how you plan to do this)*

Your Company Description does not need to be long. Keep it short and concise, and try not to overdo anything as you explain operations or how you plan to have things work. Try to keep the Company Description to more than a page but less than two pages long. Your Company Description is almost as important as the Executive Summary, because this is where you really get to pitch your goals and the uniqueness of your ideas. It's your chance to show others why they should fall in love with your company as much as you have.

CHAPTER FOUR

Market Analysis & Organization

Let's look at the next two parts of your business plan. In the first section, we are going to look at the Market Analysis and get into deeper explanations of the market results you found while researching. The second part is where you explain the structure and organization of your business.

Part 3 : Market Analysis

The Market Analysis will be one of the largest sections of your business plan. It has a lot of information to present and include, both generally and specifically, for your business. Here is all the information that you should include in your Market Analysis.

Industry Description and Future : This is a very general description of the industry you are joining. Talk about the industry's current size and what kind of growth it has seen in the past few years, as well as the expected rate of growth over the next few years. If there are any other interesting trends about your industry that you think are relevant or helpful to include here, you should do so. It's also important to include any major customer groups that exist inside your industry.

Your Target Market : After discussing the industry as a whole, define the piece of the industry that you plan to target. We stated earlier that you can't target everyone when you start out; , it's time to narrow your focus and define your target market. As you define your target, there are certain characteristics of your market that are important to mention. They are discussed below.

Classifying Characteristics : Every target market has characteristics that separate them from everyone else. Whether it's age, gender, ethnicity, job, etc., there is always a characteristic or two that separates them from others. What is it? After you've defined their unique characteristics, look at their needs. Are they being met? Do they have a need that your product or service can fill? Is there anything about this group of people that will affect your sales?

Size of Your Target Market : Now that you've decided on a target market, you can find it's approximate size. It will take a little researching, but you should be able to determine approximately how many people exist in your target market. You will also need to project whether your target market is going to grow, decline or stay the same in coming years. You should project for at least the next ten years in your business plan.

Market Share : This takes a little work, but you need to find out how much of the market is available to you. You obviously can only make an educated guess at this, but choose an area to work with and make calculations. Be prepared to back up your calculations with real logic indicating how you came up with your numbers.

To calculate market share, use simple division. You calculate the number of sales for a specific product or service (in this case, you would use the number of projected sales for your product or service). Then divide that number by the number of sales the industry has as a whole for the product or service. Multiply that figure by 100, and you have a business' market share for that product or service. Conduct a market analysis and see where your company fits in the current market and industry. Where are your customers coming from? Is there room for you in the mix?

Pricing Structure & Gross Margin Targets : In this section, explain how you plan to price your products and services. This is important and should be thoroughly researched and explained. Every product and/or service you offer should have a price, but it should also have an explanation for why you've chosen the price. So how do you price your products or services? This doesn't need to be overly complicated, but it does need to be researched and well thought out. Start with what you think your market is willing to pay for the product. This can be based on your own opinion, and it might be too high and it might be too low. You can raise and lower your price as you go, but you have to start somewhere, so give it a number. Then see what your competitors are charging for the same or similar products and services. How does it compare to what you are charging? Are you over priced, underpriced or just about right? You can consider changing your price based on what you see, or leave it and see what happens.

Choose your price based on the amount of products or services you plan to sell. This will ultimately determine your profit margins. If you are too low with your price and sell a moderate amount, you won't turn a very high profit. If you are too high and sell a few, you also won't turn a very high profit. It's all about finding a good balance.

Another consideration of your pricing structure is whether or not you are going to offer sales, bonuses, or rewards to customers. This is a very popular strategy for businesses today and definitely something worth considering as you design your pricing structure. You can establish loyalty programs or reward systems with points, gift cards, etc. The options are truly endless, but customers like to be treated well, and they will go where they feel special. When you project your gross margin target, you are looking into the future and making an educated guess about where your company is going to be in six months, a year, two years, five years and ten years. These should be realistic and informed guesses. You know that at first you will struggle and probably won't turn as much of an initial profit, if any. The most important thing is to be realistic and yet optimistic when making your gross margin target.

Keep in mind, when you reference your research during this section, don't get too detailed. You can briefly mention the research the results you found, but then you should reference your reader to the appendix, where he/she can see more detailed information about the study, market test, etc. This section is designed for you give the results rather than to expand on the details of your research and market tests..

Analyze Your Competition : The final item that needs to be included in your Market Analysis in a rundown of your competition. You should give a quick but detailed analysis of any and all companies against whom you are competing for customers. Here are some points to include in your analysis:

• Their Current Market Share

• Strengths & Weaknesses

• Is Your Target Market Important to the Competition?

As you analyze your competition, you may realize that there are some other potential obstacles you may encounter. Consider them and take some time to write down how you might deal with some of these obstacles. Here are some things you might encounter.

• Is there a seasonal market that you would like to avoid or capitalize on?

• Does your market have secondary or indirect competitors that could impact you?

• Are there other obstacles to the market (changing technology, no qualified personnel, etc.)?

Once you have finished your pricing strategy, you have completed your Market Analysis, which is the third part of your Business Plan. As mentioned, this section will be long, probably the longest section in your business plan. Don't worry too much about the length as long as you have included everything and kept your wording concise and to the point.

Part 4 : Organization & Management

Here you lay out how your business is going to be run, managed and organized. These are the questions that need to be addressed as this section is written. This section is going to include the details about ownership of the company and basic profiles for the most important people in the company, as well as the qualifications for board members (or equivalent). You may not have all of these people on staff yet, but your readers want to know as much information as possible, so provide it. If the same person does multiple jobs in your company, that's okay; just make it apparent in the business plan, and include the qualifications for that person so your reader knows why that person has the ability to do multiple jobs.

Salary and benefits for your employees should be included in this section. If you are offering any incentives for your employees, they should be listed, as well as any promotions or options. Help your reader know that these people aren't just names on a piece of paper, they are real people who are also invested into this company.

You should include in your Organization and Management a chart that helps to illustrate how the company is set up. You could easily create something similar to the illustration above, replacing the silhouettes with names, or provide a simple organizational chart to help readers understand how your company is organized.

Your company's ownership should be clearly explained in this section as well. You'll need to explain whether you've decided to be a sole proprietor, a general or limited partnership, if you've incorporated your business, and if you have, if it is a C or S corporation. All of these terms sound complicated if you are unfamiliar with them. They all involve different tax documentation and filing, as well as licensing. If you are unsure what kind of ownership you have or want, here is a great website that will explain the different types of ownership structures Business Ownership Options.

Once you've taken the time to explain the ownership structure of your business, you should outline the profile of the owner(s). Here is the information you should include for the owner(s).

- Name
- Percentage of Ownership
- How much this person is involved in the company
- Form of ownership (Partner, Sole Owner, Common Stock, etc.)

There will be other key people in the company who also should be part of this outline. They, too, should have profiles in this section. An owner may have their profile expanded through this section if their duties include doing other things in the company. Here is a list of the information you should collect from other employees in the company. (Think of it as a resume.)

- Name
- Position (description if necessary)
- Primary responsibilities in the company
- Education
- Experience and Skills
- Prior Employment
- Industry Recognition/Special skills
- Community Involvement or Community Service
- Number of Years with the Company
- Compensation or Salary
- Other Achievements, as you deem fit

If you have a Board of Directors, you should include their resumes as well, with their positions on the board. You should note that their position is unpaid and they are working in an advisory role to the business. As a start-up, you may or may not have a board in the beginning, but as you grow it would be highly beneficial to gain one.

Organizing your business is a vital piece of the puzzle, because it requires you to take everyone that is involved in the business and assign roles and. In the beginning, sometimes it is a "mishmash" of people and jobs, but as you become more organized, everyone finds a place and an assigned role in the company.

CHAPTER FIVE
Service/Product Line & Marketing

Next we are going to discuss your Service and Product Line, as well as your Marketing and Sales Management. These are two very important pieces to your business plan. As you work through these two sections, you get closer to completing your overall plan.

Part 5 : Service & Product Line

As you prepare your Service and Product Line section, you are describing what you have to offer the consumer. Here is your chance to take a whole section of your business plan and sell your product or service. Isn't that what you've wanted to do from the beginning? Here are the things you need to include in this section.

- **General Description** : First, give your reader a general and overall description of your product or service. Think about it from a customer's perspective. If they have never seen your product before, what would they want to know? Describe it to them. Talk about the current state of your product. Is it still in a prototype stage, or just an idea? What are the benefits of your product?

- **Life Cycle of the Product** : Spend a few minutes discussing the life cycle of your product. Do you offer a lifetime guarantee? When do you expect customers to buy the product again? When does it run out? How long does it last?

- **Copyright & Patent** : Have you gone through the process of patenting or copyrighting your product? Do you have any pending patents? If so, you need to list them in this section. If you are planning to get them, you also need to state that. If you have any legal agreements with any other parties regarding your products, you need to make that known here as well.

- **Research & Development** : Are you working on anything else? Is there something new on the horizon is the same industry that you are planning to introduce down the road? Entice your readers with your plan. What other research and development activities can your readers anticipate from you in the future, for this business and potentially others? This is your Service and Product Line section. It isn't very long, perhaps a page to a page and half, but it is important. It includes very valuable information for you to sell your product and entice your reader to coming on board with you.

Part 6 : Marketing & Sales Management

This section is very important, and it will also probably be a little lengthy. This is where you will outline your marketing and sales strategy for your business. If you've never been exposed to any marketing and sales before, you'll need to do some extensive research on this topic in order to feel comfortable with tactics and ideas. You can pay outside companies or individuals to do your marketing, but you'll pay dearly. The price might be worth it, however, if you cannot reach your target market and your marketer can.

As you create your marketing strategy, you are creating the strategy that is going to get customers in the door. This is how you will turn a profit and stay in business. There is no one way to do it, but there are four keys to marketing that will help make your marketing strategy more successful.

- **A Penetration Strategy** : You need some sort of strategy when you first open your doors. There are several, and you'll have to find and pick your favorite, but the important thing is that you do something that tells your target market that you are here and open for business.

- **A Growth Strategy** : This is strategy that you use to help build your business. It can be anything from franchising to buying out another business. You are simply looking for opportunities to take your business and make it grow.

- **Channels of Distribution Strategy** : This is getting your products and services out to customers. It can be through retailers, distributors, or even through your own sales team. You are simply finding a way to get your product into the hands of potential customers.

- **Communication Strategy** : This is the marketing strategy that you use to talk to your customers. Are you going to put a commercial on television? Ads in the newspaper? What about a billboard? You need to find ways to reach your customers and let them know you are in the neighborhood. Now that you have your marketing strategy put together, you can go to work on your sales strategy. The sales strategy is what takes place when the customers walk in the door.

You'll need to identify a sales strategy for your sales team. How will it work? Are you going to give the team incentives for the number of sales they make? Are they going to work off commission? Are you going to give weekly or monthly bonuses for the most successful employees? What other sales strategies are you going to use? Think about different strategies you've experienced in your lifetime. Some employees approach you and ask if they can help you as you enter a store, others don't bother you at all. Some walk you through your entire shopping trip from beginning to end. What kind of employees do you want in your business?

After you have put together your sales strategies, you have completed Part 6 of your business plan. You are ready to proceed to the next section, where you'll put together a funding request for your potential investors.

CHAPTER SIX
Funding & Financial Projections

If you are requesting funds from investors then you will need Part 7. Otherwise, you can skip it. Up until now, you have been working to impress and show potential investors that your business has the potential to be successful and turn a profit. Now is the time to actually make the request for the funding you need. The section following your Funding Request is where you will make your Financial Projections for your business in its future years.

Part 7 : Funding Request

For many people, this is what writing a business plan is all about. Although there are many benefits to writing a business plan, making your Funding Request is important. You want to make sure to get this part right. Here is what you need to include in your Funding Request.

- **Current Funding Requirement** : This is your start-up costs, plus anything else you might need.

- **Future Funding** : Outline any funding requirements that you anticipate over the next five years. Obviously this might change, and your investors are aware of that, but be as specific as possible. Try to outline the funds that you think you'll need over the next five years.

- **How the Money Will Be Used** : Allocate your funding requirements to show how the money is going to be used. You've already done this with your start-up costs, so it shouldn't be difficult to show where the money will be going. Investors want to know their money is being spent on things that are needed and truly part of the company. They don't want to waste their money, so prove to them that you will use it wisely.

- **Strategic Financial Plans** : Outline any plans you have for the future of your company that might affect your finances. These can include a debt repayment plan, a company buyout, or selling your business. They are important, because they impact your ability to repay your loan.

- **Type, Term, & Time** : You need to define for your investors what type of funding you would like, the time period your loan will cover, and the terms of the loan. When outlining each of this part of your request, be realistic. If you have no idea what kind of numbers to ask for, look online, or ask your loan officer for advice. They are there to help you. Although you won't include it in your funding request, you also will need financial information for your company. Most of this information will be placed in the next section. You'll need some historical financial information for the company; this is basic and simple for a start-up. Mainly, you'll need to be familiar with your company's prospective financial information, which we'll complete when writing Part 8.

Part 8: Financial Projections

You've put together a great business plan, and you're down to the final piece, your Financial Projections. While this piece seems simple enough, in reality, it can feel a little overwhelming. The Financial Projections portion of your business plan allows you to look down the road and make an educated guess about where your profits will be a year from now, two years from now, and so on up to five years in the future. It isn't always the easy to project. However, now that you've analyzed the market and you know more about where your business fits in the overall scheme, you have a better idea of your business' potential. Let's go through some specifics that need to be included in this section.

Historical Financial Data : This only applies if you already own an established business. If you do, you'll need to include approximately three to five years worth of data. You will need to include things like income statements, balance sheets, and cash flow statements. You may also want to include any loan information.

Prospective Financial Data : Again, investors want to see what you expect your company to do in the foreseeable future, so create charts, graphs and text that will explain and support where you think your company will be in five years. For the first year, break it down by quarter for the first year, then annually for years two through five.

You should include mock income statements, balance sheets, cash flow statements, and capital expenditure budgets. One note: creditors love to catch your projections and funding requests at odds. Catch any mistakes before they do! Don't be afraid to include graphs or charts to help illustrate your point. Although Part 8 of your business plan can be intimidating because you are making so many assumptions, try not to feel overwhelmed. Work through it piece by piece and this section will come together well.

CHAPTER SEVEN
Business Plan Appendix

An Appendix is not a required part of a business plan, although most people find it necessary, because there are several pieces of research and data that they feel add to their overall plan that don't fit or are to bulky to be placed anywhere else. If you are interested in this piece, feel free to add it onto your plan; otherwise you are welcome to skip Part 9.

Part 9 : Appendix

As noted, the Appendix isn't required, but it can include a myriad of different information relating to your overall business plan. It can be very helpful to reference it when you need to throughout your business plan, and your reader can choose to look in the Appendix for further information if he/she is interested. Another reason to include an Appendix is the fact that your business plan is going to be seen by many different people, but not everything in your plan will apply to everyone. Some documents may apply to your investors or creditors, while other documents may only be important to potential employees.

You want the documents easily referenced for appropriate readers, but you may not want everyone to have to look through all your documents. The Appendix is a great way to accomplish both.

Here are some documents that you may include in an Appendix:

- Credit Reports/History (personal & business)
- Resumes
- Product Pictures
- Letters of Reference
- Market Studies
- Licenses, Permits, Patents
- Copies of Leases
- Building Permits
- Contracts

Your Appendix is a great place to keep information, as well as share information with others.

CHAPTER EIGHT

Helpful Forms & Other Online Resources

Writing a business plan isn't easy, and it takes a lot of time and patience. There are some great online resources, templates and websites that others have put together to help you as you write your plan.

- *Entrepreneur.com* has put together several great templates to help business owners get started. You can download their templates into a Word document and customize it to fit your own needs.

- *Bplans.com* has sample plans that you can look through and work with to help create your own business plan. They even have different categories of sample plans, which will allow you to find a business plan that is going to be the closest to your own. These are a great resource for you to see how other business owners have crafted their plans and put together their information and research. Bplan.com has put together a site full of business planning calculators that it boasts will help you through the business planning process. It has a calculator to help you with cash flow, another for start-up costs, even a calculator for email marketing. This is a great website to help you with the calculation portions of your business plan. BPlan Business Planning Calculators

- *Smarta.com* also has over 500 sample business plans that you can reference as you are writing your own. Their plans are excellent resources, and they seem to have a business plan for just about any business imaginable. Smarta is also partnered with a Business Planning Software company, Live Plan, which you can download (for a fee), and use to write your business plan.

- *Kickstarter* is one other helpful website that has put together a great list of business tools for you to use as you get started. They have just about anything from tax estimate and 401k loan calculators to expense reports and finance statements. It's a great website to help you keep track of things and make projections.

All in all, there are many online resources available for you. Jump online and see what you can find to help you if you are discouraged or stuck in a rut.

CONCLUSION

We really hope that the information provided in this book was valuable to you and that it met or exceeded your expectations. Customer satisfaction is extremely important to us so if for any reason you are not satisfied with your purchase, have comments or feedback you would like to share with us, please send us an email at *info@clydebankmedia.com*.

Additionally, if you would like a refund for your purchase, you can return the book through Amazon up to a certain amount of days from the purchase price. If you would like a refund please email us at *support@clydebankmedia.com* and we will happily refund your total purchase price.

Finally, if you enjoyed the book we would love to receive a positive review from you on the book's product page. Thank you!

ABOUT CLYDEBANK BUSINESS

ClydeBank Business is a division of the multimedia-publishing firm ClydeBank Media LLC. ClydeBank Media's goal is to provide affordable, accessible information to a global market through different forms of media such as eBooks, paperback books and audio books. Company divisions are based on subject matter, each consisting of a dedicated team of researchers, writers, editors and designers.

The Business division of ClydeBank Media is composed of contributors who are experts in their given disciplines. Contributors originate from diverse areas of the world to guarantee the presented information fosters a global perspective.

Contributors have multiple years of experience in successfully starting and operating online and offline businesses, marketing and sales, economics, management methodology and systems, business consulting, manufacturing efficiency and many other areas of discipline.

For more information, please visit us at :

www.clydebankmedia.com

or contact us at :

info@clydebankmedia.com

MORE BY CLYDEBANK BUSINESS

Etsy Business For Beginners

How To Build & Promote A Profitable Etsy Business

Visit : http://bit.ly/etsy_business

Agile Project Management QuickStart Guide

A Simplified Beginners Guide To Agile Project Management

Visit : bit.ly/agile_quickstart

Scrum QuickStart Guide

A Simplified Beginners Guide To Mastering Scrum

Visit : bit.ly/scrumguide1

Agile Project Management & Scrum Box Set

Agile Project Management QuickStart Guide

& Scrum QuickStart Guide

Visit : bit.ly/agileprojectmana

Lean Six Sigma QuickStart Guide

A Simplified Beginners Guide To Lean Six Sigma

Visit : bit.ly/lean-sixsigma

Project Management For Beginners

Proven Project Management Methods To

Complete Projects With Time & Money To Spare

Visit : bit.ly/project_success

Copywriting Mastery

Exactly How To Become A Professional Copywriting Expert

& Create Content That Gets Attention & Sells

Visit : bit.ly/CopywritingMastery

3D Printing Business

How To Get Rich From Home With 3D Printing

Visit : bit.ly/3dprinting_rich

eBay Business For Beginners

Exactly How I Make A Six Figure Income With My eBay

Business And Why It Is Easier Than You Think

Visit : bit.ly/ebay_rich

Etsy Business For Beginners

How To Build & Promote A Profitable Etsy Business

Visit : bit.ly/etsy_business

Etsy & eBay Business Box Set

Etsy Business For Beginners & eBay Business For Beginners

Visit : bit.ly/ebay_etsy

Made in the USA
Middletown, DE
22 May 2015